Better Management Skills

This highly popular range of inexpensive paperbacks covers all areas of basic management. Practical, easy to read and instantly accessible, these guides will help managers to improve their business or communication skills. Those marked * are available on audio cassette.

The books in this series can be tailored to specific company requirements. For further details, please contact the publisher, Kogan Page, telephone 071-278 0433, fax 071-837 6348.

Attacking Absenteeism
Business Etiquette
Coaching Your Employees
Consulting for Success
Creative Decision-making
Creative Thinking in Business
Delegating for Results
Effective Employee Participation
Effective Meeting Skills
Effective Performance Appraisals*
Effective Presentation Skills
Empowerment
First Time Supervisor
Get Organised!
Goals and Goal Setting
How to Communicate Effectively*
How to Develop a Positive Attitude*
How to Develop Assertiveness
How to Motivate People*
How to Understand Financial Statements
Improving Employee Performance
Improving Relations at Work
Keeping Customers for Life
Leadership Skills for Women
Learning to Lead
Make Every Minute Count*

MARKETING
FOR
SUCCESS

MARKETING FOR SUCCESS

Tony Fletcher and
Neil Russell-Jones

**KOGAN
PAGE**

Acknowledgements

The authors gratefully acknowledge the assistance of Susan Hughes, for her useful advice and helpful suggestions arising from her review of this book.

First published in 1994

Kogan Page Limited
120 Pentonville Road
London N1 9JN

© Tony Fletcher and Neil Russell-Jones 1994

British Library Cataloguing in Publication Data

A CIP record for this book is available from the British Library.

ISBN 0-7494-1254-2

Typeset by BookEns Ltd, Baldock, Herts.
Printed and bound in Great Britain by Clays Ltd, St Ives plc

Contents

About This Book

Marketing for Success is intended to be read and used. It includes case studies, work sheets, diagnostics and questionnaires which will encourage you to think about the subject under discussion and illustrate the general approach that may be taken.

By using the book, that is reading and completing the examples, you will be able to gain an understanding of marketing techniques and develop your own plan of action using those techniques, which we hope will enable you to increase your sales.

The book presents an overview of marketing as it is applied in industry, retail, commerce and, increasingly, in the public sector. It covers all the major areas of marketing. Some of the techniques mentioned will be the ones that you want to use, and others will not. You must therefore use the book selectively and choose those aspects that suit you. A select bibliography for further reading is included.

The concepts and techniques presented should be taken on board and *used* in your business, as appropriate. The questionnaires and diagnostics have two purposes:

- To test your understanding of the concepts and to assist that understanding
- To enable you to take them away and use them in your business on a day-to-day basis.

The key areas that this book concentrates on are:

- *An overview of marketing* – to enable you to understand what marketing actually is and (perhaps more importantly) what it is not. It examines products, services and distribution and provides examples of where and how marketing went wrong, highlighting the pitfalls.
- *Finding out about your customers* – to demonstrate why you need to know about your customers, and how to do this. It examines the different types of market research and when and where to use them.
- *Strategy and planning* – to explain the need to put a marketing plan together and to help you to produce your own marketing plan. Guidance is given as to what it should contain, such as timings, costs, milestones, actions and measures of success.
- *Putting the plan into action* – To demonstrate the practical aspects of marketing, that is the elements of what is known as the 'marketing mix', and to illustrate some typical campaigns. Advice is also given on longer-term planning.

The case study concept
Throughout the book, in order to illustrate some of the points about marketing in the context of practical business decisions, we will use three mythical companies: one each in retail, manufacturing and service industries, to develop situations to enable you to think about marketing concepts or ideas:

The three companies

Alto Speakers. Employing 90 people, Alto manufactures a range of technologically advanced loudspeakers used primarily by hi-fi enthusiasts and in recording studios. The products are sold through specialist hi-fi dealers.

Stratos Consultants. Employing 20 professional staff, Stratos provides management consultancy and training services, mainly to smaller and mid-sized companies.

Cirrus Retail. With 40 high-street sites, Cirrus retails two distinct types of product:

- Hi-fi separates (amplifiers, cassette decks, CD players, speakers, etc) through 15 of its shops
- Computers and software through the rest.

Where relevant we use real life examples to illustrate the marketing actions taken by businesses which have been successful or, in some case, failed spectacularly.

In the text we often refer to 'consumers'. By this we mean the general public who purchase goods and services (items such as a pair of shoes, clothes, food and drink, white goods such as washing machines, banking, insurance and plumbing services, holidays, travel, etc). Those who provide the goods and services are taken to be businesses and include partnerships and sole traders as well as 'middle men' such as wholesalers, unless specified to the contrary.

CHAPTER 1
Introduction

What is marketing?

It is worth starting with a definition of marketing, as many people have preconceived and often erroneous ideas as to what it is, and what it is for.

Write below your definition and understanding of the term marketing.

_____

_____

_____

_____

_____

_____

_____

_____

There is a definite benefit to be gained from marketing, provided that is done effectively. We shall attempt to show you how in the following pages.

What follows is our preferred definition of marketing, and some others for comparison.

The following definition is very clear and precise and encompasses the key elements:

'The function of sales, distribution, advertising and sales promotion, product planning and market research. That is those functions in a business that directly involve contact with the consumer and assessment of his needs, and the translation of this information into outputs for sale, consistent with the firm's objectives' *Penguin Dictionary of Economics* (1978)

Other definitions include:

(a) 'Marketing is the management process responsible for identifying, anticipating and satisfying customer requirements profitably', as defined by the body which represents individuals in marketing in the UK – The Chartered Institute of Marketing.

(b) 'The aim of marketing is to make selling superfluous': Drucker, P (1973), *Management: Tasks, Responsibilities, Practices*, Harper & Row, New York.

(c) Adam Smith, the famous 17th century Scots economist and author of *The Wealth of Nations* (1776) said: 'The sole intent and purpose of production is consumption', by which he meant that the only reason for producing something is for it to be used, that is by a consumer.

(d) 'Marketing is matter in motion': Converse, P, Heugy, H and Mitchell R (1958) 6th edn, Ch 1.

(e) 'Marketing is simply sales with a college education': John Freund, quoted in *Great Business Quotations*, 1985.

(f) 'Marketing is common sense with buzz words': business studies mythology

(g) The average marketing professional would say marketing is 'the process of matching the resources of the business with customer needs, profitably' (note the use of the word profitably).

As a final thought you might consider that in the USA marketing means going to the supermarket to pick up groceries.

The marketing cycle

The marketing cycle, on page 14, shows the key components of the marketing process. We will examine each of these elements in turn:

- *Market research* – finding out what the customer needs (Chapters 4,5), as well as conducting an *internal analysis* of the business
- Establishing a *marketing strategy* – what are we going to do? (Chapter 6)
- Putting a *marketing plan* together – how to do it (Chapter 7)
- *Implementation* – doing it (communication with the customer) (Chapter 8).

You will note that the process starts and ends with the customer, the person or organisation that purchases your goods and services. This is because marketing is concerned with finding out what the customer needs and then trying to satisfy those needs.

It is now useful to look at some examples of where marketing has been applied successfully and where it has not, to place the rest of the book in context.

Successes

Marketing people talk about products, brands or services to describe what they deal in:

- A **product** is a manufactured item (for example, a machine tool, an umbrella or a chocolate bar).
- A **brand** is the name that an item or group of items is marketed under (Ford, Toyota, Barbour, JCB, Dryzabone, Cadburys, Pepsi, Coke, Levis).
- A **service** is the supply of (usually) people-based services (consulting, banking, insurance, travel, estate agency, car valeting, medicine, dentistry).

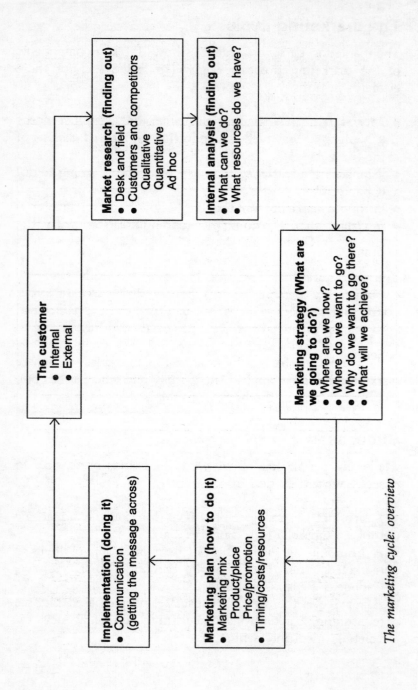

The marketing cycle: overview

List below some products, brands, or services that, in your opinion, have been successful and your reason for this success. Examples of success could mean excellent advertising campaign, quality image, fit for needs, well designed for the purpose, or well priced.

Product	Reason for success
_____	_____
_____	_____
_____	_____
_____	_____
Brand	
_____	_____
_____	_____
_____	_____
_____	_____
Service	
_____	_____
_____	_____
_____	_____
_____	_____

Some examples for you to consider:

Motorcycles. In 1960, if you wanted a cheap and efficient way to commute to work, you would have gone to see your local Triumph, BSA or Royal Enfield dealer to buy a motorcycle. Just ten years later you would have gone to a Suzuki, Honda or Yamaha dealer instead. These companies, by virtue of good product design, pricing and astute marketing virtually wiped out the British motorcycle industry. This did not happen in the UK only. Few producers outsider Japan managed to stay in business in the face of this onslaught, and even though some developed successful niches (Harley

Davidson in the USA and Moto Guzzi in Italy) they are not large players, although fairly profitable.

The fax. This device, invented for military and meteorological purposes over 40 years ago, and latterly developed for Japanese domestic use, only took off in the mid 1980s for international commercial use. Now how could we live without that document faxed over the Atlantic/across Europe?

The personal computer. This book was written on a portable machine that is more powerful than some main frames used in the late 1960s. It is not just a case of technology, but also of affordability and application. Consider whether PCs would have been as successful without the software to drive them (for example, Lotus, Word Perfect, Windows), high-quality printers (laser and bubble jets), and the industry standards imposed by companies such as IBM and Apple. Currently we are in another phase of PC war with prices tumbling and ideas such as the 'notebook' (a PC that fits inside your briefcase) and a PDA (personal digital assistant − a pen-based computer) are all the rage. IBM is reckoned to have 'won' the war in the 1980s (fighting back against Apple) but who will win in the 1990s?

Failures

We can all think of recent examples of products and services which have 'bombed' in the market place − perhaps due to poor design, wrong price, insufficient quality, etc.

List opposite those which spring to mind as recent (ten years or so) failures and more importantly why they failed:

Product	Reason for failure
_____	_____
_____	_____
_____	_____
_____	_____
Brand	
_____	_____
_____	_____
_____	_____
Service	
_____	_____
_____	_____
_____	_____

A straw poll of some of our marketing colleagues came up with the following:

Sinclair C5 (UK). No demand for an impractical product aimed at the wrong market. (It should be noted, however, that one entrepreneur snapped up the unsold stocks of this product and by astute targeted marketing managed to sell them at a profit.)

Betamax and Philips 2000 (Europe). The technological advantages were insufficient to justify the purchase of two or more video formats and they lost out to VHS.

Ford Edsel (a car) (USA). Ford misread the market and is reputed to have lost $350 million – largely from promoting the product as a new innovative car, which was in fact not the case and, in its haste to get it to market, Ford allowed quality control to slip, effectively killing the product.

If you have not heard of any of these this rather underlines the point.

It is important to remember that, as much as anything, marketing is a state of mind, and must permeate the whole organisation to ensure success: if the sales representative does not understand, or is not committed to, the ideals of the company it does not matter very much what the managing director says or does. Similarly, the first point of contact, often a telephonist or a receptionist, is part of the marketing team and contributes to the image of the company and its products and services.

We can all think of companies where we have spoken to an employee who has not been interested in your call, be it a complaint or an order. We can also think of those where the opposite is true and where staff are keen to go out of their way to help. Examples of the latter would include in the USA and internationally, McDonald's, some airlines and hotel chains, or in the UK, John Lewis and Marks & Spencer. If you asked your customers for their comments what would they say?

Staff commitment comes through an understanding of the marketing ideals of the company; participation, in some form, in the development of marketing plans and initiatives; and from training and explanation. As an example look at British Airways (BA), which transformed itself from an unpopular, unprofitable nationalised industry in the 1980s to the 'World's Favourite Airline' in the 1990s, as well as one of the few profitable airlines in the world.

Similarly British Telecom (BT) which since it was privatised *and* subject to competition (Mercury and mobile phones), has become a much more customer-led organisation.

As an increasing number of countries privatise their state-owned companies market forces are having an appreciable effect on those companies. In the USA, where competition has generally been more fierce historically, service has been given a much greater emphasis and has influenced the marketing process accordingly.

The process of change can be time-consuming (BA took 10

years) but the payback is enhanced sales and therefore profitability, happier customers, satisfied shareholders and fulfilled management and staff.

Marketing is not, however, a science and mistakes are made – would you wish to be remembered as the person whose idea it was to market a new version of Coca-Cola in a manner that almost ruined the company and saw its share price plummet? No, you would rather be remembered as the person responsible for marketing Cabbage Patch dolls, the mobile telephone, Teenage Mutant Turtles, lap-top computers, or in 1993 the resurgence of Thunderbirds and of course Jurassic Park.

CHAPTER 2
Overview of Marketing

As already mentioned, marketing can be broken down into four main components:

- *Research* (finding out)
- *Strategy* (setting objectives and goals)
- *Planning* (steps to achieve goals)
- *Implementation* (doing it).

The application of any one component in isolation is not effective, although the techniques can be considered separately.

Research

This means finding out both about yourself and about your customers and starts with an internal look at your organisation (often called an 'audit') to identify:

- What your company is good at
- Your **strengths (S)** and **weaknesses (W)**
- The **market opportunities (O)**, and
- The **threats (T)**.

(Collectively, often called a **SWOT** analysis.)

Then you must find out what customers need (*market research*).

When this has been done you can match the two. This will give you a *gap analysis* — the difference between what you are offering and what your customers need.

You then have to take action to *close this gap*.

However, when it comes to marketing, you very rarely start with a clean sheet. You have production lines, you have staff, you have budgets, etc, so you have to aim, not for the perfect fit, but for the best *practical* fit to your resources.

In many ways marketing is about positioning and packaging your product or service to make the most of it — but it must be fit for the purpose.

Above all else marketing is about understanding the consumer of the goods and services you offer. In essence it is about understanding what these people *need* and what they *want* — and there is a big difference here. It is then about providing this in a form that is attractive. Compare caviare and fish eggs — one and the same thing except that people pay hundreds of pounds for one and next to nothing for the other. Similarly with Kiwi fruit — a hairy, green, unknown New Zealand fruit that gained a surprising popularity through a sophisticated marketing campaign.

Strategy

This sets the goals and objectives for the business and involves questions such as:

- Where are we now?
- Where do we want to go?
- Why do we want to go there?
- What will we achieve?

In setting the strategy the research previously conducted should provide the answers to these types of questions. Once the strategy, that is the direction, has been set you then have to answer the next question: How do we get there?

Planning

Marketing planning answers the question, 'How do we get there?' and can be summed up as getting the right mix of the key elements – the four Ps:

- *Product* (or service)
- *Place*, also called location (distribution, availability)
- *Promotion* (how the product/service is presented to the consumer)
- *Price* (what to charge).

These, essentially, are simple ideas – what is it, where can you get it, how do you tell people about it and what does it cost? It is common sense really, but it is often ignored, overlooked or forgotten.

Consider the following:

Product. This is what you are selling and you must make sure that it matches the customer's needs. You may have only one product/service, or a few, and for larger firms the numbers may run to five figures, but there must be a plan for each item to ensure that you maximise your return. Sometimes products or services are grouped together for marketing purposes. These are known as 'lines' or brands. For example Procter and Gamble or Unilever will have several types of detergents and they will be grouped as a 'line' because they share characteristics, customers, distribution or price ranges. The collection of lines is known as product width, and the number of items in each line as the depth. The closeness of characteristics is known as the product consistency. These three – width, depth and consistency – have implications on strategy as a company tries to compete.

Place. It is often said that there are three key concepts to selling your product or service: location, location and location. Why is the rent for retail property so much higher on the high street or in a shopping centre or mall, than on a back street? If you want to supply the whole of the UK would you site your store in Scotland, Cornwall, or Nottingham? Where would you site yourself to serve the whole of Australia or the USA? Why do banks pay a premium to get an address in Lombard Street (in London), or Wall Street (in New York) and retailers an address in Oxford Street (London), Avenue Louise (Brussels), Fifth Avenue (New York) or Ginza (Tokyo).

Because there is a benefit from the best location. For a shop, passing trade is more frequent, for a warehouse, distribution is easier or, for a service company, communications are better. Sometimes a prestigious address can add to the perception of your products or services (UK tailors in Savile Row). The key message is to make sure that your product or service is available where people want it, when they want it.

Promotion. This is how you present the product or service to your customer, and includes packaging and design as well as advertising. Much research is carried out into promotion, but you are simply trying to make the item appeal to the customer and meet his or her needs. Packaging can be very important, whether it is the colours of the box or the brochure, or the shape of the container. Consider Avon Cosmetics where one-third of its products are repackaged every year to ensure that they continue to appeal to customers. Some of the packages have become collectable, so great is their appeal.

Advertising also has a large part to play in this aspect but it does not always work. Perhaps the most famous of all promotional gaffes was a brand of cigarettes called Strand whose advert depicted a lonely man on a bridge at night, smoking in a contemplative manner. Many consumers thought that he was a social outcast or was going to commit suicide. They deserted the brand and it is no longer with us.

Advertising

At this point it is worth explaining where advertising fits in to the picture. Many people – wrongly – equate, marketing with advertising. This is because it often represents the 'sharp end' of the campaign, that is the communication to the customer. The two are not the same and in fact advertising is only one part of a marketing campaign. It comes *after* you have carried out your research and decided on the position, place and price etc.

Now consider the following case study:

Case study

The managing director of Cirrus has been out to the Far East and has come back having signed a deal to take 5000 PCs with very high specification sound and picture capabilities. These PCs can also show a conventional TV picture in part of the screen (so you can watch *Neighbours* while using your spreadsheet!). He asks his managers to set up a low cost TV campaign to run just before Christmas.

What steps would his managers take?

Naturally enough, being marketing professionals, they were not pleased about this unplanned purchase (the elements of research, strategy and planning being absent) but they applied their professional skills to the task and:

- Calculated a budget for the promotion (following internal guidelines)
- Selected an advertising agency (not forgetting that an element of sales promotion in store would also be required)
- Prepared a brief for the agency
- Looked at the creative suggestions provided by the agency
- Got the agency to book space on the TV (aimed at an agreed target market)
- Had the advertisement made and then screened for a test audience to check its relevance and suitability
- Put in place a system to monitor the effect of the advertising, to see how cost effective this type of promotion was.

Price. The decision on price is important. The two ends of the spectrum can be described as 'pile it high and sell it cheap' at the bottom of the market sometimes called 'every day low price' (EDLP), and at the top of the market as a sophisticated product for which people will pay more, for example luxury goods such as Cartier or Rolex watches, Burberry coats and many perfumes. What is the difference between the jeans you buy in a market and a 'designer' pair? The answer is price and perception of value for money (which may of course reflect quality – perceived or real – or a desire to be seen with that particular good). Price alone therefore is not the determinant factor for purchase. There are many examples of products which purportedly sell more as the price goes up (the Rolls-Royce is often quoted in this respect due to the snob appeal or social cachet attached to it).

The price will also affect the demand. You will sell more at a lower price than at a higher one, generally speaking, but you must make sure that the price covers costs and leaves a margin for profits. There is also the question of what can the market bear? A 5 per cent uplift in the price of champagne may not have too much effect on sales, but a 5 per cent increase in the price of a family saloon in an intensely competitive car market could be disastrous!

As an example, in late 1993 the price of *The Times* newspaper was cut in an attempt to boost revenue. While this may sound odd it is, in fact, rational because the economics of newspapers are driven more by advertising revenue than by price. A price cut is expected to boost sales which should lead to increased advertising revenue, which is based on the number of people reading a publication. There may also be an ancillary objective of forcing competitors out of the market by starting a price war. The USA experienced just such a price war in the cigarette industry during 1993/94 with a wholly unexpected cut in the price of Marlboro. This was completely contrary to previous statements by the company which produced it (Philip Morris) and led to a fall in its share price of 10 per cent in one day (called Marlboro Friday). This decision was taken, however, because Philip Morris realised that

Marlboro, a premium brand priced accordingly, was losing market share to cheaper rivals and they therefore had to cut the price to maintain (and perhaps enhance) market share.

The policy chosen, however, can lead to problems. It can take a long time to rid oneself of a cheap image. Tesco (the giant UK retailing chain) spent a lot of time and effort in moving itself upmarket in the 1970s. Once a brand acquires a cheap image many people do not buy it for fear of association in the mind of their peer group. Japanese car manufacturers have successfully moved themselves into the luxury car bracket with many of their products, having initially positioned themselves as cheap cars to 'buy' market share.

When marketing, it is important that the four Ps are applied consistently in order to ensure that your goods or services continue to appeal to purchasers. The market is littered with brands that have disappeared because these four essential factors were overlooked or mismanaged.

Implementation

It is no good having a plan to achieve your strategy based on excellent research if you do not do anything about it. To make your marketing a success the plan must be put into action. You must get your message across to your customers and potential customers.

Imagine that you are a customer of your own company and write down overleaf what improvements you would suggest or want, under the four Ps, − be honest.

Product

_____
_____
_____
_____
_____

Place

_____
_____
_____
_____

Promotion

_____
_____
_____
_____

Price

_____
_____
_____
_____

In order to achieve these changes and to put your plan into action _you_ must take action. This means you need to find out about your customers and make a plan for changing your marketing to match their needs. This is dealt with in the following chapters.

CHAPTER 3
An Introduction to Market Research

So, what is market research? It is a very simple concept based on the idea that if you find the customers' needs and wants and then use the information to provide a package that meets these, then you will be successful.

It was an understanding of needs that led to the establishment in the UK of Sock Shop by Sophie Mirman. She had experienced the frustration of women who buy a lot of stockings or tights but very rarely got a wide choice from shops, or the shops were not conveniently sited, or were not open at convenient times for working women. By meeting the need of such women for a wide range of this type of goods in convenient locations (for example, railway stations) which were open when working women could get to them, she launched one of the retailing successes of the 1980s.

Similar ideas in the UK included Tie Rack and Knickerbox and in the USA Victoria's Secret, a retailer of exotic and luxury underwear, which was a great success after it realised that by making such garments fun it created a whole new market.

There are, however, many techniques that can be used to ensure that you find out what the customers need. Consider the following case study:

Case study

Alto has been producing its low-range loudspeaker in a teak case, with a conventional black grille (acoustically transparent front). The company has noticed a trend towards hi-fi units that are all black in design, with a rather 'high tech' appearance, and thinks that a redesign of the speaker might prove popular with customers.

There are a number of options that it can choose:

- A black case with a similar front as before
- A black case with no acoustic screen, thus showing the speakers themselves
- A completely radical design that does away with a conventional cabinet altogether.

In this case the company would do the following.

First the company should carry out some desk research to look at sales and trends of equipment currently in the marketplace. For example it could review competitors' advertising over the last six months (by looking in the major magazines) and it could also review their sales literature.

Following this a series of telephone calls to buyers at major retailers should elicit more information.

However, if the new product is going to be revolutionary (rather than evolutionary) then Alto will have to undertake some direct market research.

The company would probably prepare mock ups of the different options and then hold some group discussions of people in the target market. It could complement this with some face-to-face interviewing (in stores) of people who were about to buy speakers.

It might carry these actions itself or perhaps partly or wholly through a market research agency.

There have been many failures of market research, with perhaps the most notable recently (in the UK) being the failure of pollsters to predict the outcome of the 1992 General Election. Given that they only had to ask a simple question at the exit polls — how did you vote? — you might be forgiven for thinking that it should be easy to get the right answer.

Why was this? Well in this case the jury is still out. Was the sample wrong? Were the questions worded in a misleading or biased way? (Until the result came in almost all commentators were convinced that the Conservatives were going to lose and interpreted any data to support his view.) Or did people simply lie to the researchers? We may never know, but it does serve to show that even simple concepts have their pitfalls. (Datsun once produced a car called the Cedric, based on faulty research that purported to show that this was a popular name in Australia.)

If you work in a large enough office you may like to try the following exercise:

Ask your colleagues if they are left-handed, using the statement:

'I am carrying out some research around the office and would like you to tell me if you are left-handed.'

When they have answered the question ask them the following:

Do you write with your left hand?
Do you play sports with your left hand or a mix?
Do you eat with your knife in your left hand or in your right hand?
With which hand do you throw?
With which hand do you catch?
To which ear do you place the telephone?

It is certain that you will receive answers at variance with each person's answer to the first question. Why is this? Think about this and write down your reasons.

```
┌─────────────────────────────────────────┐
│                                         │
│   _____│
│   _____│
│   _____│
│                                         │
│   _____│
│   _____│
│                                         │
└─────────────────────────────────────────┘
```

Now compare your reasons with our answer. The question 'Are you left-handed' is not specific enough as there are degrees of left-handedness. Consequently, everyone puts their own interpretation on the question (normally the hand with which they write − but not always so) and therefore the answers are somewhat biased. If you really did want to know with which hand people wrote you would use a question that was more specific such as 'With which hand do you write?' Even here you will get ambidextrous people who may give answers which may distort the results.

This shows how careful you must be in choosing both samples and questions. To avoid this kind of problem a number of techniques are used. The most obvious is the split between answers which are precise and measurable (quantitative) and those which are more subjective expressions of an individual's opinion (qualitative).

We will look at these in more detail in the next chapter.

In case you are interested people who are left-handed are called sinister (from Latin − the term for right-handed is dexter − ambidextrous means both hands right-handed) and comprise around 10 per cent of the population as a whole. This proportion is, however, higher in groups that have received further/higher education, and in samples of people with mathematical/logical leanings such as those who work in computers and management consultancy. There is clearly a market for left-handed products such as golf clubs, guitars, pens, scissors, hockey sticks. (Both authors are management consultants who are left-handed and have often found themselves working in teams where all members were left-handed − a situation which happens infrequently in life.)

CHAPTER 4
Finding Out What Your Customers Need

What people want and what they need are often two very different things, and an understanding and awareness of this difference is critical when carrying out market research.

For example:

- You or your neighbours have just been burgled and so you **want** increased security at your home but do you **need** a burglar alarm, or grilles on the windows, or a guard dog, or do you **need** better locks?
- You **want** to be entertained for two hours so you **need** to visit the cinema (or do you **need** to read a book or get a video)?

Asking what people want will lead to some very wide-ranging answers; many people *want* a Rolls-Royce or a Ferrari, but you would be in deep trouble if you tried to use this information to judge the actual level of demand, as their wants will be very much ahead of their pocket, and is their real *need* for transport of some sort or just a status symbol? Even if you ask them what they need it may not necessarily give you any idea of how to provide it or even how they want it provided.

The development of the Sony Walkman is a good example in this respect. Asking people if they wanted 'music on the move' 20 years ago would have elicited blank looks, but asking them if they wanted to be entertained on public transport, on the beach or jogging would probably have received a 'yes' but given no clues as to how to meet this need.

While the above may appear to be a semantic nicety, it is in fact very important because, when carrying out market research, you must be absolutely sure that you are addressing the right issue.

List below the products and/or services that *you* provide and, for each, why your customers *want* them and why they *need* them.

Product, brand or service	Want	Need
_____	_____	_____
_____	_____	_____
_____	_____	_____
_____	_____	_____
_____	_____	_____
_____	_____	_____
_____	_____	_____

The difference between *wants* and *needs* can sometimes be crucial, and for many customers it cannot easily be explained. You must therefore find out the difference by structuring any questions accordingly. The answers will enable you to make sure that the products and services you are offering meet your customers' requirements.

Fuji Photo Film carried out some research into the market for cameras and found that customers were bored with new, expensive, sophisticated products and instead wanted convenience at very low prices. This led to the introduction of the phenomenally successful cheap, disposable camera.

It would have been impossible for Fuji to discover this information if it had not carried out extensive and wide-ranging research. Rather than perhaps focusing on extensions to its existing range, it focused on the reasons why people want and need a camera.

We will now move on to consider the different research techniques that may be used.

Research techniques

There are two main types of research, *desk research* and *field research*, but there are several ways of carrying them out.

Desk research

Before starting any market research it is appropriate to ask: 'Has it already been done by somebody else?'

Within most countries an enormous amount of research is carried out every day. Some of it is confidential and never published, but much of it ends up in the public domain, through research reports, directories and other types of documents. Many research reports are often released to the media where they form the basis of stories, articles, features, etc. There are usually central directories in most countries that list market research reports which are available through libraries.

List below the major sources of information, of which you are aware, that might contain information that could be used by you in your business.

```
┌─────────────────────────────────────────────┐
│                                             │
│   _____    │
│   _____    │
│   _____    │
│   _____    │
│   _____    │
│   _____    │
│   _____    │
│   _____    │
│   _____    │
│   _____    │
│                                             │
└─────────────────────────────────────────────┘
```

A brief (and generic) list of the major sources is as follows:

Major sources of information

- Trade associations and professional bodies (these often have very relevant industry sector information)
- Market research companies (Gallup, Advertising, AGB, MORI, Neilsen are some of the larger UK firms)
- Government statistics (in the UK the Central Office of Information and HMSO)
- Commercial publishers of market research (Keynote is one of the larger firms)
- Providers of company information (*Who owns Whom?*, Extel, Dun and Bradstreet)
- Directory publishers (Kompass, Thomson)
- Trade journals (look especially for surveys)
- The press (a search can often reveal interesting articles about published surveys, which can in turn lead one to the original source).

For many people the easiest way to carry out desk research is by visiting their local library, or for more detailed information visiting one of the more specialised libraries. Many universities and business schools, for example, have excellent libraries (always ring them in advance to find out about what they have, how to gain access, etc).

A subscription to an electronic database or CD ROM system can also be a useful investment, as they allow you to carry out comprehensive searches rapidly (albeit at a cost).

An alternative is to get professional help by, for example in the UK, contacting the Market Research Society for a list of members specialising in your sector and then asking for advice and quotes for assistance.

Field research

Whereas desk research is finding out what has already been discovered in your sector by others, field research, is by contrast, *finding out for yourself.*

There are many different ways of finding out what people's wants and needs are. List below those, if any, with which you are familiar.

Now compare yours with those in the following list:

Main types of field research

- Telephone research
- Written questionnaires
- Street interviewing

- Face-to-face interviewing
- Product tests
- Consumer panels
- Focus groups

Key points

Before undertaking research of any kind there are some key points to bear in mind:

(a)	The sample	Who are you going to ask?
(b)	The method	How are you going to ask them?
(c)	The questions	What are you going to ask them?
(d)	The results	What will you do with the information?
(e)	The cost	How much do you want to pay for the answer?
(f)	The time-scale	By when do you need the information?

In the following pages we consider each of these in turn.

The sample

The number of people questioned is very relevant to the research, as the more that are asked, the more likely that the answers will be close to reality. Does this mean, then, that you have to ask everyone who might buy your product or service to obtain an accurate idea of what the answers should be? If it did you would have to spend a lot of time and effort in asking potentially millions of people questions. Fortunately, the answer is no, as a lot of research has been carried out in this area by mathematicians (statisticians really) and the result of this research includes the following truism:

> If you ask enough people the same question, after a certain point, no matter how many more you ask, the percentage difference in the answer does not vary significantly, or if it does the margin of error can be calculated quite accurately (for example within 95 per cent certainty).

What this means is that you do not need to question

everybody to find out what the answers are, you only need to ask a 'statistically significant number', and generally you can be sure of the answer, subject to the degree of error (plus or minus 5 per cent) which you can take into account.

This number is surprisingly small, although it has to be calculated for each circumstance. For example, for election forecasts the number chosen is in the region of 2000 – carefully chosen to be representative of the population as a whole. By contrast for consumer (that is ordinary people) and industrial products the number is usually in the low hundreds.

The people you will want to find out about are known as the 'population'. This does not mean the whole of the country, however, merely those people likely to be interested in your goods or services. In some cases the 'population' can be large (a whole country/state/county), and in others it may be small (say, for example, swimming pool owners) in one town.

The number of people asked the questions is known as the 'sample'.

In order to get an accurate picture then the research must be carried out over an homogeneous range of people within this 'population' (that is groups with the same characteristics). This breaking down of people into such groupings is known as segmentation, and is important not only in market research but also in targeting customers.

Segmentation

Segments usually reflect the groups at which marketing communications, products, etc are aimed, and therefore it usually makes sense to carry out market research in corresponding segments to be targeted. In some circumstances it can be difficult to determine exactly what is the appropriate segment and sometimes initial research is carried out to assist in this.

The segments commonly applied in consumer research are:

Age
Sex
Income
Location
Type of dwelling
ACORN (A classification of residential neighbourhoods)
Education levels
Marital status
Family or not
Social group
Lifestyle
Religion
Culture

Typically, the market research would focus on those segments that were most appropriate to the products or services being sold.

In many cases segments are cross-correlated with others (called sub-segmentation) to narrow the field. For example, people over 55 years old living in 'high-value' neighbourhoods might be targeted with retirement products thus avoiding wasting time and money on those not interested in such items, or having little disposable income.

Much of the information used in targeting consumers is obtained through lifestyle surveys, manufacturers providing information to third parties, on products that they have supplied, from product registration cards and through subscription databases such as *Reader's Digest* or *Time-Life*.

List below the segments that might be appropriate for your products or services.

The method

We have already mentioned the major methods above, and in the following pages we give a brief explanation of each.

Telephone research

Quite simply this is ringing people up and asking them for their views. It is, however, much more difficult than this. People are not well disposed to unsolicited calls, and will often not speak to you, or fob you off with a set of phoney answers to get rid of you.

Why then use it? Well, if properly carried out:

- It is relatively cheap
- It can be very focused (although you cannot research people who do not have telephones)
- It is fast.

Key points

- There should always be a structured question script (This does not mean that it should be read word for word but it should act as an aide-memoire and the important points should be ticked off to ensure that they are covered.)
- Tell the interviewee the company name, then yours and then the purpose of the research, without giving away anything which may be prejudicial to the answers. You can always give them more details at the end but do tell them before you begin that you will do this.
- Tell them how long the call will take (don't lie as this really upsets people).
- If you are researching companies take the name, department and title of the person to whom you are talking, in case you want to get in touch later on or to check that they are senior enough to represent the views of the company adequately and accurately (you might get the office junior).

NEVER MIX UP RESEARCH AND SELLING!

This is called 'sugging' and is not only unethical, it is usually very unproductive. It may also lead to a string of complaints. The Market Research Society, for example, has a set of ethical guidelines for all research and these are well worth looking at.

Written questionnaires

This is a very common method of research, and is familiar to most people. Some examples are the questionnaires in:

- Hotels – how did you enjoy your stay, what did you think of the room or service?
- Banks – was the counter service quick enough, were the staff pleasant?
- Magazines – how many people read your copy, which articles did you enjoy most?
- Aeroplane in-flight questionnaires or those handed out in airports.

This method can provide useful detailed information but it is a passive way of surveying customers. Not many people return them, unless they are part of the checking-out process in an hotel, or there is an incentive. It also tends to highlight the negative as those customers with a grievance are more likely to return them.

Sometimes gifts are given out, or prize draws and other means (for example, Air Miles) used to encourage responses. This sort of research tends to be expensive and should only be entered into where the cost/benefit has been considered and found to be favourable.

Written questionnaires can be either quantitative or qualitative (or a combination) and they have considerable advantages and disadvantages over some other methods. For example, if you were stopped in the street and asked 'How much was your last electricity bill?' most of us would reply £30 or £50 or some other guess. If you received a written questionnaire at home, however, you will probably look up the answer and put £37.56 or whatever.

A key disadvantage is that where a long answer is required the temptation is to paraphrase and thereby omit salient points.

Key points

- This method is subject to the 'can't be bothered' factor and to receive a good enough sample you may have to send out up to 20 times the number you need (a 5 per cent return is considered good).
- The ease with which it can be filled out is also important, as this impacts on the return. Usually questionnaires are tested first by sending out a trial sample. This allows you to test the ease and quality of response.
- People tend to return questionnaires more frequently when there is a pre-paid envelope enclosed, and where there is a stamped addressed envelope the return rate is phenomenal as people hate to throw away a stamp. (This is however, much more expensive than pre-paid envelopes as you must pay for every stamp in advance, unlike pre-paid envelopes where you pay only for returns.)
- Length is crucial. Most people will prefer to complete and return a short pithy, well-designed questionnaire, rather than one which has 30 pages of closely typed script.
- The quality of the targeting will be reflected in the returns. A letter addressed to 'B Walker Esq', 'Miss A Bloggs CVO', or 'Dr J K Smith', is much more likely to elicit a response than 'Dear Sir/Ms/Madam', etc.
- Questions must mean something to people. 'How long was your holiday?' is unspecific and the answers will be largely useless as people will not know which holiday, whether to count travelling time, etc.

Write out below a specific question about one of your products or services.

_____

_____

_____

_____

Now get five people to answer it, and compare their answers with what you expected, looking for any ambiguities or problems with wording and whether you can make sense of the replies.

Street interviewing

This is also known as quota sampling. Usually interviewees are stopped in the street and asked a few personal questions, before going on to a second series of questions or being told thank you, that's all. This is because the interviews have been designed to be statistically significant, and the sample is segmented prior to the questions. (For example, the interviewer has been told to interview 50 males between 18 and 25, 30 females between 18 and 25, 20 'professional' males, 10 males in 'blue collar jobs', etc.)

The initial questions are, therefore, *screening* the interviewees. Thereafter the technique is similar to telephone interviews, except that it is possible to use visual prompts to aid answers:

- Which colour do you prefer? (shows colour chart)
- Which pack design do you find most attractive? (shows examples)

This technique is almost always used in consumer research, as it is of little help in business to business. (It might be fun, though, to stand outside an investment bank and ask, 'Have you borrowed £10 million, £30 million, or have you made a hostile bid for a company recently, etc.)

Key points

- Segments must be wide enough to be practical – if you picked males under 30 with red hair and brown suits, there might not be enough people to stop and interview.
- Questions must be short as people are being stopped in the street without prior appointments and may only have a little time.
- There should not be too many locations as this can be very expensive because of the cost of the number of people required to ask questions.

Generally, using professional companies yields better results as they can use a number of techniques to ensure that people are not alienated or threatened by being stopped, but if you do it yourself then:

- Be courteous
- Always approach people from the front, in a bright light and signal your intentions clearly from a distance
- Politely accept no for an answer
- Prepare a quota sample and ensure that you progress through this as evenly as possible (you don't want to be standing out in the rain looking for the last red-headed man to make up your sample)
- Ensure that the questions are simple, unambiguous and above all that you can analyse the answers you get
- Take no more than 10 minutes or so
- If appropriate have something to show to interviewees (do you prefer this colour of this one?)
- Provide some kind of reward for their time (even a cheap biro with your company name)
- Have an umbrella handy if it looks like rain.

Face-to-face interviewing

This takes the form of a structured conversation, and so all the cultural conventions of conversations apply. If at all possible you should provide the interviewee (who, in a business, is likely to be a middle manager or above) with an agenda for the discussion *before* the event. A good idea is to fax or write with the agenda and at the same time confirm details of the meeting.

It is quite common for interviewers not to say for which client they are working (this is to avoid building any prejudice into the interview), and to give more details after the interview. At the very least the interviewee should know how to contact the interviewer after the event in case there are any further points.

The interviewer will normally have a one- or two-sheet guide to the questions that he or she wants to ask, and these should be ordered so as not to give too much information to interviewees, thus prejudicing their views. The interviewer should always ask permission to take notes or to record the interview. Tape recording can put people off as it can be obtrusive and inhibiting, therefore, in most countries, it is not currently much used for market research (although it is extensively used for journalists' interviews).

Key points

- Confirm the interview beforehand with a letter or fax
- Arrive on time, and make sure the interview doesn't overrun
- Guide the conversation gently, but firmly
- If the interviewee is not forthcoming then thank him or her, make your excuses and leave
- It is normal to follow up the interview with a thank you letter
- People are giving you their time and therefore you must be prepared to give them something in return, usually in the form of extracts from the findings (in a non-attributable form) later.

Product tests

This type of research is widely used, particularly, but not only, in consumer markets. It involves getting potential customers to try a product directly and to report back on it. One method is called the 'hall test' as a local village hall often provides a convenient place to set up a product testing site.

One type used by manufacturers, however, is the direct consumer test, whereby new or improved products are sent to members of a panel for trial.

This is used frequently, for example, in the confectionery industry where new chocolate bars or biscuits are often tested in this manner, and it provides valuable feedback. It is not really appropriate, however, to send out some products for comments, owing to the cost involved (Rolls-Royces, for example) and a different method of research would be used.

An interesting example of product testing that has come to the fore in recent years is in the software industry. As computer software is very complex it can be expensive for developers to test, and so they select sites (called beta sites) which receive early versions of the product free of charge, in return for providing detailed comments about its performance in practice before final release.

This process has become much devalued in recent years as the commercial pressures on software developers have led the less scrupulous among them to release these beta products direct to general customers, let them complain about bugs and then produce a new version that fixes these. Unsurprisingly some products have now developed a reputation for being rushed out without being finished. Think how you might feel if your new car was delivered with an experimental wheel fixing and the company asked you to report if it worked properly.

Key points

- Choose an appropriate place to hold the tests (for example, for food outside or more frequently inside a supermarket, for audio equipment in a large area such as an exhibition hall)

- Make sure that everyone who participates is given a questionnaire to complete
- Ensure that those testing the product represent the target market
- Circulate during the event to get 'off-the-cuff' remarks and record these for later analysis.

Consumer panels

Consumer panels (also called Omnibus surveys) are also widely used. This is where pre-segmented panel members complete a diary on a regular basis. The diary usually consists of two parts:

- A regular section where they may be asked to note when and where they bought the products or services covered by the survey; and
- A special section which manufacturers buy into on an irregular basis. This may be used to ascertain the results of certain promotions, advertising campaigns, etc.

The panel members are usually recompensed by gifts, purchasing points or maybe air miles.

The panels can be structured to reflect particular segments, or samples, and tend to be a very cost effective method of getting information, however, they are rather limited by the written format. If products or services are not fast moving, then they may not appear as entries in the diary very often and will provide insufficient data. For example, you might include newspapers, visits to fast-food outlets, soft drinks, but probably not lawn mowers, cars or PCs.

Key points

- Use a specialist firm
- This is for fast-moving consumer goods (FMCG) only.

Focus groups

These are also called group discussions and are just that. They are a specialised form of face-to-face interviewing and are mainly used in assessing consumer views but are equally valid in assessing industry views from groups of managers.

The format is as follows:

1. An audience of between 6 and 12 people with selected backgrounds are invited to the meeting. This takes place in a room designed to be comfortable and put people at ease (like a drawing room).
2. A moderator or facilitator (often using visual aids) explains the purpose of the focus group and may give some background to the topic.
3. The group is then invited to discuss the relevant issues. The discussions are usually tape or video recorded (or notes are taken by an assistant).
4. The moderator guides the discussion to make sure that it stays on the subject.

The purpose is to get a set of people from selected backgrounds (usually similar) to talk in a directed way about one or two topics. Where it differs from conventional interviewing is that as the group talks among itself it can often spark off radically new ideas or concepts that have not been considered. They are commonly used at the beginning of research campaigns to ensure that the detailed exercise covers the relevant points.

A common format for industry groups is the 'Heaven and Hell' concept where participants are asked to imagine those two scenarios in their sector/industry; they are usually quite revealing.

Key points

- Ensure that the audience represents the desired segment(s)
- Make sure that the audience is relaxed and participants feel free to speak
- The quieter members of the group must be encouraged to speak as well (a key role for the facilitator)

- The quality of the moderator and his or her skill in developing the discussion and thereby the results is key, and specialist firms are usually employed (especially in the consumer industry) to maximise value from the exercise
- Sometimes the participants are paid, and at other times a dinner is provided to relax participants. The latter is common in groups looking at industry trends. A free lunch however is not the same as a structured focus group.

The questions

Before engaging in research you must ensure that you know what you want to get out of the exercise and, therefore, what you want to ask about. The method of research will also affect the way in which the questions are structured. Written questionnaires require a different format from interviews and telephone questions.

There are two types of questions – **quantitative** and **qualitative**.

Quantitative types are easier to answer and easier to analyse. They ask for specific data. You usually ask the subject to fill in one box from several. Thus:

Do you buy baked beans?   YES or NO

or

How many tins did you buy this week?   1,2,3,4 more? (specify)

The answer is clear but of limited value, except to tell you that they do or do not buy baked beans and in the latter case the amount. It therefore requires many more questions to arrive at the information sought. When do you buy them? How often? Where? What do you pay? and so on.

Qualitative questioning is much more difficult to analyse as it allows the person answering it to describe how they feel. Thus:

'What do you think about baked beans?' or 'How do you like to eat baked beans and what with?'

For many people expressing themselves in writing is much harder than verbally and, as it takes more time, they do not always give a full answer (for example they may say they like baked beans on toast but omit to mention that they never buy them because the rest of the family hate them).

To obtain precise answers you must make sure that the questions are:

- Unambiguous
- Answerable concisely
- Comprehensive
- Open to analysis.

Questionnaires frequently fail this test, thus rendering the data collected useless or meaningless.

The more quantitative that questions are, the easier it is to undertake analysis leading to robust conclusions. It can often help to give a series of options for answers to help the respondent in articulating his or her answer and to facilitate analysis.

The best answers usually arise from a combination of the two.

Tips
Where you are carrying out research in more than one country, or in a foreign language it is important that all answers are ticks in boxes and not sentences, otherwise you are subject to vagaries of translation and interpretation of both questions and answers as well as cultural differences. (In the UK for example the word 'redundant' means of no further use but in the USA it means spare).

It is important to get the translations agreed to your satisfaction well in advance of sending the questions out and this can be time-consuming (as the authors have found out from bitter experience).

The order of the questions is also important, as a previous question can influence a following answer.

Q1   Do you buy:
     Brand 'X' beans;
     or
     Brand 'Y' beans;
     or
     Brand 'Z' beans?
Q2   What is your favourite brand of beans?

The questions are in the wrong order as the first gives clues to answering the second. The respondent may have forgotten about Brand 'X' but may be prompted to give a false answer to the second question.

Measuring answers
Precise questions can be easy to think of, but the answers themselves may not get you very far. For example, the question 'Which newspaper do you prefer – *The Times* or *The Independent*?' might appear to be a precise question but it is not, and you would have to be prepared to accept a lot of answers. Write down the answers that you might get.

_____

Now compare your answers with our sample answers:

> *The Times*
> *The Independent*
> Neither
> Don't know
> Both the same
> Never read papers
> I'm Spanish and don't read English

You can, however, ask the same question in a different way:

'On a scale of 0 to 5 (with 0 being not at all and 5 being very much) how do you rate: (a) *The Times*; and (b) *The Independent*?'

This is a comparative question and would help you to find out which of the two people preferred, but not why.

A more sophisticated form of comparative questioning is often used when companies wish to know the trade-offs (usually against price) that consumers might make. It is called **conjoint analysis** and might take the form of a series of questions:

Would you prefer your car to have either:

- A CD player or a sun roof?
- Air conditioning or be £500 cheaper?
- Air bags or anti-lock brakes?
  and so on.

The market researchers can then ascertain the comparative value that consumers place on each feature. A computer program is usually required to work out the detailed results from the response, but well-designed research can actually tell you the comparative values that consumers place on items.

This type of research is not appropriate to all types of business, and its use is dependent upon the way products/services are sold.

The results

The key question to consider when commissioning or carrying out market research is: 'What do I intend to do with the results?' That is, why do you need this research?

Market research can be very expensive and so it only pays to collect information on those areas that will be of direct use to you in furthering your business and developing your marketing. While it is always nice to know as much as possible about what your customers think, if the information is not relevant you do not need to collect it.

The best method to ensure relevant output is to list all the answers that you want the research to provide the facts for. You can then use this list to check that completed questionnaires will supply the information you require.

You will be surprised at how many research surveys ask questions that seem relevant and pertinent, but when the researchers come to analyse them they cannot extract useful information from them.

Example

One of the things that Alto Speakers needs to know is whether consumers of its products prefer to be able to mount their speakers vertically or horizontally. If it asks the question: 'Which way do you prefer to mount your speakers: vertically or horizontally?' people will give one preference or another, but this misses out those people who can't express a preference or might want to do both, and thus may be very misleading. The question should accordingly be better structured to catch the possible permutations.

It is also important to put any caveats or reservations into the report alongside the results, so that when managers are reading the report they are not drawn into false conclusions. You may be familiar with the remark that there are lies, damned lies and statistics; people are easily misled by figures, and often no more so than by reading a figure in a report that says that '90 per cent of people prefer brand X to brand Y' (but missing the small print that says 'out of the 10 people we asked' or 'who expressed a preference').

In reports, even if you cannot gauge the statistical accuracy, it is a good idea to use some common sense, especially if the sample is small, or if the results are erratic or they appear to differ widely from other surveys or results.

The cost

The cost of market research can vary widely from a few hundred pounds to the many millions spent by multinationals on major consumer brands.

It is relatively easy to assess the cost of market research and the procedure to follow is:

- Estimate the component activities that you think will be needed (100 telephone calls, 20 face-to-face interviews, etc)
- Assess the amount of time input that this requires (see below for a guide)
- Identify the daily cost of either your own staff or employing people of the right calibre to do the work. (Typically researchers cost between £150 to £300 per day, although senior staff used for carrying out high-level, face-to-face interviews can cost a lot more.)
- Add in the preparation time for questionnaires and the time to analyse and write up the reports.

Only you can be the judge of whether the cost is warranted or not, and although excessive market research is certainly wasteful, undertaking no market research at all is likely to be an even bigger risk (and perhaps cost) in the long run.

Guide to researchers' time
Telephone calls: a typical telephone research call takes 10 to 20 minutes, but don't forget that the researchers will have to ring many numbers to get through to callers who are prepared

to participate, they have to write up the calls afterwards, and they may have to search for numbers, etc. As a guide, think that around 8 to 10 completed calls per working day will be a good result.

Face-to-face interviews: these are much more time-consuming as the researcher has to travel to the interview, which may take some time as well as the actual duration of the interviews. The researcher has to set up the interviews and write them up, which can be quite complex. Typically, only two face-to-face interviews can be accomplished in a day, and if travel to other towns is required, then this may fall to an average of one and a half.

Street interviewing: Generally, higher production rates than telephone interviews will be achieved because the interviews, although usually the same length, are normally written up as they go and the interviewees come to the researcher (although it may take time to find individuals who match the quota sample). Thus around 20 to 30 per day may be accomplished.

Group discussions: These take some considerable time to set up and although the group will only meet for between one and four hours the transcripts and analysis may take a lot of time. Set aside at least a day for administration and a half day for the group. Don't forget that usually more than one person is required to run a group interview.

Written questionnaires: It is generally a good idea to construct written questionnaires so that the answers can be transcribed directly from the forms on to a PC to facilitate the analysis of results. In sending out a written questionnaire there is a considerable amount of secretarial/administrative support required such as developing the mailing list, preparing the letters and posting them (this is called 'fulfilment' in the trade jargon). Percentages vary widely but, typically, a response of between 1 and 3 per cent is considered normal: thus if you want 100 people to reply, you may have to send out between 3000 and 10,000 questionnaires, and you should not underestimate the time and effort in doing this! Response rates can be raised by telephoning people or using a variety of other techniques (for example, reply paid envelopes, free gifts, good personalisation, etc).

The time-scale

To arrive at the time-scales involved in research one usually works backwards from when the results will be required to estimate the probable start date.

The most appropriate way to calculate the time-scales for carrying out market research is to produce an activity chart (sometimes called a Gantt chart). This shows the various steps, their time to completion and the interrelationship between each of them. An example is shown on page 58.

Typically the stages will be as follows:

Estimate/scope the project: decide what type of answers are needed and how to go about getting them.

Set-up phase: this may involve hiring contractors, preparing the questionnaires, developing the samples, purchasing mailing lists, etc.

Desk research: this involves searching existing information for ideas, pre-existing surveys and background data that could be useful to develop the full-scale research.

Test phase: sometimes called piloting. Questionnaires are tested on a small sample of people to check that they give the right answers, are consistent, etc.

Research: this may consist of a number of phases, one leading to another: for example, consumer research to test preferences, followed by research into trade intermediaries.

Analysis: at the end of the research it is appropriate to analyse the results and check that all the objectives have been met.

Reporting: all market research should culminate in a written report for the benefit of others in your firm, subsequent publication if appropriate, and to provide a reference document for later activities.

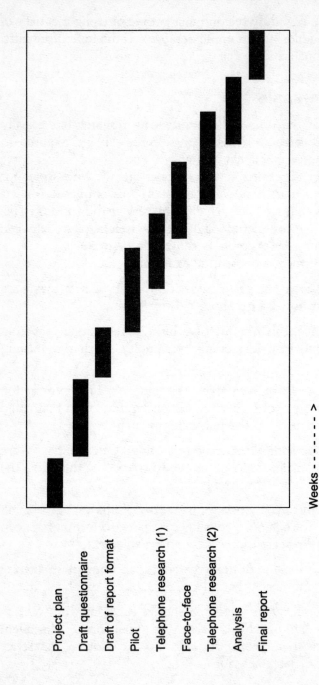

Project plan

Draft questionnaire

Draft of report format

Pilot

Telephone research (1)

Face-to-face

Telephone research (2)

Analysis

Final report

Weeks - - - - - - >

A Gantt chart: typical research project plan

The time taken to carry out market research varies widely, depending on the scale of the research and the type of research being carried out. It is also appropriate to consider the time of year: business-to-business research carried out in the summer and across the Christmas period or other similar periods (Yom Kippur, Ramadan, Easter, Chinese New Year, etc) is usually much slower as many of the intended interviewees are away on holiday and take longer to get to see.

The moral here is: plan well ahead, you should expect some problems and should try to anticipate them.

CHAPTER 5
Strategy

Once you have undertaken the market research and analysed the results you must then develop your strategy – that is, what you are going to do. You must also write it down – a strategy that exists only in your head is not a strategy at all.

For your marketing to work you must have an idea of:

- *Where* you are going
- *Why* you are going there
- *What you will achieve* by getting there.

This is called the **strategy**. It does not cover *how* you will do this as this is contained in the **plan** – we will consider the plan in the next chapter. (It is common, however, for a document to be produced containing both a strategy and a plan because, although they are separate items, they are closely interrelated.)

Any business has a reason for its existence. This holds true for one-person outfits through to giant multinational companies, and for profit-making entities and non-profit making ones (for example charities). In order to operate successfully the business must put its overall company strategy together which will define what the company does, why and for what reason.

Consider the following: you want to go to Scotland to see your aunt to deliver something to her and to collect something from her. This (although you may not consider it in these terms) is a strategy, as it says *where* you are going, *why* you are going and *what you will achieve*.

It does not, however, contain the details of the *how* (the journey). You could go by train, fly, drive in your car or go in a hired van or lorry. What leads you to decide the how will be driven by several factors: the size of the item for delivery and that for collection, the time-scales involved, the relative costs, etc. The plan will lay out these details — often called operational or tactical — following your consideration of the factors and research into conditions which will affect putting the idea into action.

A marketing strategy, by comparison, concentrates on the marketing aspects of the business, but must of course be in sympathy with the overall business strategy.

A strategy should also look further than a plan, usually three to five years out, whereas a plan will normally be concerned with the shorter term (for a business plan, one year is usual).

Consider the following case study:

Case study

Alto Speakers has received a cash injection through the sale of some peripheral assets and is in a position to invest in an extra production line and/or to increase marketing expenditure. Should it:

1. Expand existing facilities;
2. Build a new line for a new range of lower cost domestic quality products; or
3. Move into an entirely new market for studio quality loudspeakers?

To answer these questions Alto must consider its strategy and how these choices best fit with it, and conduct a SWOT analysis of its operations to provide relevant input for its decision. It may also need to carry out or commission some market research. Only when it has the right information can it make a decision.

The new line (if it goes ahead with this option) would have to be planned in the context of existing operations – it would be an unusual step for a company making a range of low-quality cheap products suddenly to move upmarket unless this is an integrated part of a transitional strategy towards longer-term goals.

The goals would have to be appraised and thought through, and perhaps altered to reflect and meet what the company perceives as the market needs.

Market analysis

In setting a strategy it is imperative to look at the market in which you are operating. A company that defines itself in terms of its own products will not be as successful as one that has examined the market and defined itself with reference to that market. For example, a business that defines itself as selling LP records will soon find itself missing out as the market shifts towards CDs, DAT (digital audio tape) and DCC (digital compact cassette), possibly videos, and succeeding new products, compared to one that defines its objectives as satisfying customers needs for music (or even entertainment) and therefore, recognising the trends, adapts as the market changes.

To set the correct marketing strategy it is necessary to carry out this analysis of the market in a structured manner. You must, therefore, consider the following:

Market characteristics (what is the market like)

- Economic trends
- Competitive structure
- Market size
- Technological changes
- Regulation
- Products or services.

Your **market position** including

- Your market share
- The bases of competition in your markets
- SWOT analysis
- The key success factors.

By combining these you get your **market situation** which is an analysis of the market characteristics against your position within the market. This tells you where you are and what you need to do within your market.

When you add in your **internal condition** (your overall strategy, your resources, and your operational capability – that is, what you can do and what you want to do) this leads you to see what your **marketing strategy options** are. The diagram 'Market analysis', on page 65 illustrates this.

You will than be able to decide what your marketing strategy will be and this will allow you to go forward and put the plan together. The strategy will not normally be concerned with details, but will take a high-level view (macro) of business marketing, with a longer time-scale. It must of course be reviewed periodically and whenever there are major changes to factors which affect its underlying assumptions.

The plan which will support the strategy, however, must contain the level of detail necessary (micro) to enable your marketing to be successful (Chapter 6 deals with this aspect.)

Marketing risks

Risks are always associated with every action, from simple daily actions such as crossing the road to more complex activities such as building a new factory. Marketing is no exception and it is particularly relevant to consider risk when new products are to be launched or new markets are being entered. Most businesses want to increase product sales and increase penetration in markets, but must be very careful in so doing to ensure that they understand the implications.

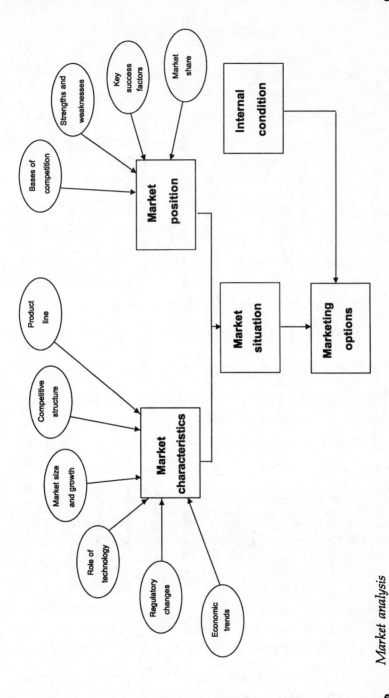

Market analysis

	Existing products	New products
Existing markets	1. Market penetration *Low risk*	2. Product development *Higher risk*
New markets	3. Market development *Medium risk*	4. Diversification *Highest risk*

Type of action

		Where the company is looking to increase sales by:
1.	Market penetration	Increasing current product/service sales in current markets by better marketing
2.	Product development	Developing new products/services for its current markets
3.	Market development	Taking its current products/services to new markets
4.	Diversification	Developing new products/services for new markets

Marketing risk assessment: product/market expansion grid

Each company must look at its opportunities and consider the key marketing risks for each.

A marketing risk assessment grid (or matrix) is shown in the diagram 'Marketing risk assessment' on page 66. This diagram plots market risk against product risk and enables the comparative risks from possible courses of action to be assessed. Those in quartile 1 are generally the least risky for a business, those in quartile 4 the most risky and the others fall somewhere in between.

You must remember that just because something is risky this does not mean that it should not be undertaken. On the contrary, most big opportunities are inherently very risky or at least more risky than the normal course of business. What is important, however, is that the risks have been considered thoroughly and steps taken to minimise them, through proper research and robust analysis into markets, consumers and the company's ability to carry out the venture, as well as thorough planning.

Consider the following series of marketing opportunities:

Stratos consultants wants to offer more consulting services and is thinking of doing the following:

A Offering its cost reduction methodology, developed in the building society industry, to banks
B Offering that same methodology to manufacturing companies
C Moving into environmental consulting.

Alto wants to expand and has discovered the following opportunities:

D A UK radio manufacturer wants it to make speakers for its radios
E A South American firm wants it to open a factory making television components in Brazil
F One of its UK customers wishes it to make microphones.

Cirrus is looking to increase the sales throughput and has the following ideas:

G Starting to sell records, tapes, CDs and videos

H   Buying a car dealership chain which is coming on to the market at what one of the directors considers is a very good price

I   A joint venture with a 'white goods' manufacturer that wants Cirrus to sell its electrical goods

J   Buying a similar company to itself with twelve outlets, which is for sale, and has offered itself to Cirrus.

These ideas are plotted on the Marketing risk assessment matrix, on page 69, to give you an idea of the marketing risks of each.

Finally, do not be put off by the term 'strategy'; the document may only be a few pages long but will help you, your employees, your suppliers, purchasers and financial advisors to have an idea of your future direction, which will help them in looking at your business.

Do test that the strategy is meaningful, however, and that it can be translated into a plan of action. Use crisp statements such as: 'We will increase the market share of product x from 8 to 12 per cent by end 1996' and 'Three new services will be launched within our superior brand line by July'. Avoid bland statements such as: 'We will be the best supplier of paper in the Asia Pacific Region', (although this type of statement is useful as a summary of the mission statement providing it is following by a statement as to 'how').

Before going further, for your own business, write out the key strategic objectives you wish to achieve, such as:

Our market share for ... (product/service) will be ... (%) by ... (date)

Our profit target for ... (product/service) will be ... (currency units)

New products/services for this year will be ...

I want my business to have the following characteristics in three years' time ...

	Existing products	**New products**
Existing markets	1. Market penetration A J *Low risk*	2. Product development F C I *Higher risk*
New markets	3. Market development G B D *Medium risk*	4. Diversification H E *Highest risk*

Marketing risk assessment matrix

Marketing opportunities – answers

CHAPTER 6
Marketing Planning

In this chapter we will help you to draw up your own plan of action for marketing.

As mentioned in the previous chapter, a plan is the means by which you as a company or, indeed an individual, are going to achieve your objectives (that is, those goals that you have set yourself).

The function of a marketing plan is to ensure that a business will hit its sales targets, thus generating the income necessary to fund the business. It is also to give guidance on how this is to be achieved and to provide a cohesive structure to any marketing activities.

Marketing supports the operations of the organisation and is not an end in itself.

What marketing is *not* is an exercise that is carried out half-heartedly by rote on an annual basis, wasting time, with the resultant document put on a shelf to gather dust. It should be a guide to actions and referred to frequently.

The marketing plan

Why do you need a plan?
We referred to this in Chapter 5 when we stated that it answers the question how do I get there? To help you further

understand this we list below the reasons why a marketing plan is necessary.

Reasons for having a marketing plan include:

To provide a framework for the people in the organisation in relation to marketing.

To act as a tool that can be used to assess progress.

To inform everyone involved of their responsibilities, activities and financial guidelines.

To persuade your superiors (and juniors) that the organisation is on a planned rather than random path.

To identify anticipated events and be prepared for them.

To maximise co-ordination and pulling together.

To minimise the chance of every one 'doing their own thing'.

To maximise the cost effectiveness of your company's effort.

To provide formal input to other company planning processes (for example, the business plan, the IT strategy, etc).

To give guidance to your contractors (advertising agency, PR company, etc).

We have now established why you should plan. The following case study illustrates what can happen when there is no plan.

Case study

When the accounts department at Stratos Consultants was preparing the budget for the coming year, the sales manager told it that he thought there would be quite a lot of business coming in from the sale of consulting services to the retail sector next year: about £2 million he thought.

What he didn't tell them was that he was going to

have to spend considerable amounts of money on advertising, sales promotion and on hiring new staff. He also neglected to mention that some of the staff working on the retail sector would be taken off environmental work, and so revenue in that area would go down.

The net result was a set of financial projections that looked very good at the beginning of the year, were presented to the bank and shareholders and widely praised. At the end of the year, however, even though the targets for sales to the retail sector had been met, the others were not. Expenditure ran out of control, and it was a different story.

The sales manager has learnt the value of planning and communication, and is now being very systematic about looking for a new job.

Other key questions are:

- What should be in the plan?
- Who should produce the plan?
- When should it be produced?
- What can be done to make it effective?
- How is this measured?

What should be in the plan?
In our view it must contain the following sections.

1. Executive summary
2. Market analysis
3. Objectives and goals
4. Marketing tactics
5. Action programme, including responsibilities
6. Budgets
7. Milestones and controls
   Appendices

It need not be a mighty tome, merely long enough to address the relevant points (typically 12 to 15 pages). If it is too long it can become difficult to digest. Try to include all major points, however, even if they are just bullet points.

You will notice that the third section deals with objectives and goals. These relate to the objectives put together in the longer-term strategy, but as mentioned before this is interrelated with the plan and forms part of the document. The rest of the plan is set in the context of these objectives and is the means of converting them into goals.

Who should produce it?

The plan should be produced by those people responsible for carrying the plan out, within an overall co-ordinated framework. A plan produced in isolation without the involvement of those in the field is just an academic exercise and is likely to fail.

When should it be produced?

The plan must be produced far enough in advance of the period to which it relates so that it is ready and agreed in time, but close enough so as to be relevant. It is usual to produce the plan towards the end of the financial year so as to fit in with the overall annual company plan and be ready for the next financial year.

How to measure effectiveness?

The effectiveness of a plan can only be measured when milestones and controls have been input in advance and agreed by those staff with responsibility for it. (See '7. Milestones and controls', below.)

A framework for constructing your marketing plan

In order to give a framework that you can take away and use, key topics that would normally be covered in each section are outlined below.

1. Executive summary

This is a very short section (1 or 2 pages). It gives an overview of the plan and is useful for helping senior people in a larger organisation to understand the key issues, or it will serve as a quick reference for smaller organisations. Detailed back-up information should be contained in the main body of the plan.

2. Market analysis

In this section the factors which affect the business are described. It should contain the SWOT analysis referred to in Chapter 2, as well as a forecast of the market, including trends, consumer behaviour, competition, segments and, if relevant, the sales history of the organisation over the last five years. (If you are only at the start-up stage you will not have a history.)

The forecast should focus on your expected sales in your market with your products/services). Threats would be such items as new competition/entrants to the market, impending changes to legislation or new products.

3. Objectives and goals

Here you should describe what you want to achieve. In larger organisations these must fit in with the higher-level plans of the firm. In smaller firms these may be one and the same. By giving *objectives* size (magnitude) and deadlines they become *goals*.

Examples of objectives could be:

- Gain market share
- Increase turnover
- Improve pre-tax profit
- Maintain return on capital.

By giving them size (magnitude) and deadlines these can become goals, namely:

- 10 per cent overall market share by end 1995
- 5 per cent increase in company turnover annually over the next three years

- Pre-tax profit of 20 per cent by next year end from 10 per cent revenue enhancement and 7 per cent cut in costs
- Return on capital of 35 per cent.

Within these goals however there may be different goals for different parts of the organisation. Some parts may have to achieve significantly higher targets than others to attain the overall targets. For example a 10 per cent increase in market share for the firm as a whole may require: 35 per cent increase in product 'Y'; 10 per cent increase in product 'X'; and no loss in product 'Z'.

4. Marketing tactics

This part of the plan outlines the tactics for achieving the goals, that is, *how* you will do it. There are three key elements to this:

(a) **Target markets** – to whom will you be selling your products and services and on whom will you be focusing? (For a retail bank, for example, this could be high net worth individuals or individuals with funds under management, whereas for a manufacturer of baby clothes it could be young couples or grandparents)

(b) **Marketing mix** – this section describes the key points, and especially concentrates on the four Ps:

  - **Product** – what your products (or services) are
  - **Place** – availability in the market place (distribution, merchandising, etc)
  - **Promotion** – how the concept is presented to the consumer (advertising, sales promotion, public relations, etc)
  - **Price** – What to charge.

(c) **Marketing expenditure** – how much will be spent on marketing and when. Different products need different levels at different times. In some markets where there is virtually no difference between products (usually referred to as commodities) consumers have to be persuaded that one is better than another. Perfume and soap powder are good examples of this. Some goods need a lot less expenditure because consumers either flock to buy them (they are 'in fashion') or they are necessities (look at the success of 'own branded' goods in the big high-street supermarkets which are marketed as 'value for money').

Some marketing is aimed at creating or expanding a market rather than satisfying existing demand. A good example would be diamonds, where De Beers controls the market and repeatedly markets the well known phrase 'A diamond is forever'. Some expenditure is largely seasonal, for example, fireworks, and you can always tell when Christmas is near in the UK from the adverts for British sherry.

Holidays are a good example of where demand for a service has moved from being very seasonal to virtually all year round. This has been driven largely by demographic factors such as less annual factory shutdowns, but also greater availability of different types of holidays (venture, skiing, activity, etc) and increasing leisure time.

5. Action programme

This should describe what is necessary to put the plan into action. It should contain tasks and sub-tasks and allocate the activities within each to a member of staff who will be responsible for them. (In smaller firms this may well be the same person.) Deadlines should be set, such as:

- Conduct market research during autumn, report due by 30 November
- Select a new advertising agency by end of February
- Book TV space for Christmas campaign by mid March
- Pilot test new product by June
- Prepare campaign for new product 'A', ready for its launch in the UK in September and Europe in the following May.

6. Budget

Many people groan when this word is mentioned; but it is a

vital part of any plan. A proper budget allows the limits of expenditure to be set in advance (which gives some freedom of action to marketing managers), fits into the overall company forecast and allows monitoring of progress to take place, as well as providing control on purchasing, resource scheduling and cash flows. It also allows you to measure expenditure against results for effectiveness.

7. Milestones and Controls

The plan must contain adequate information to allow proper control to be kept over marketing activities. This is done through:

- Establishing the budget as mentioned above
- Agreeing milestones (things that must happen by a set date to allow other things to take place logically and sequentially) for major events during the year and throughout campaigns
- Providing timely management information for managers to allow them to monitor progress on a regular basis, against milestones
- Taking action to put the plan back on course if deviation occurs.

Now consider the following case study.

Case study

Stratos Consultants currently lets the majority of its professional staff carry out the selling and marketing work on an ad-hoc basis. The managing director thinks that there may be considerable economies and efficiencies if a discrete sales force was set up and a marketing manager recruited. He asks one of his directors to draw up a plan on this basis for the next year.

What would be the chapter headings of this plan?

Would this be a marketing plan?

The chapter headings would be:

- Executive summary
- Objectives and goals
- Marketing and selling channels
- Marketing tactics
- Action programmes
- Budgets
- Milestones

This would contain most of the information of a marketing plan, but the tone of the document would be slightly different as it would concentrate on the marketing and selling channels.

To help you further with your marketing planning, here is a detailed checklist of subjects that should be covered. When you have written your plan, go through it and tick off each topic. If any are missing ask yourself why, and then, unless they are not relevant, go back and put them in.

Check list

Market analysis	
Overall market characteristics	
Size and value and expected evolution (change)	
Product/service segments	
Relative weighting (importance) of segments	
Seasonal fluctuations	
Regional differences	
Distribution networks	
Names of your products and those of leading competitors	

Product description	
Sales history	
Decision making methods	
Relative strengths and weaknesses	
Problems and opportunities	
Customer listing	
Competitors	
Objectives and goals	
Long-term and short-term	
Defined targets	
Marketing objectives (including market share)	
Company objectives	
Profit	
Corporate image/reputation enhancement	
Sales targets	
Marketing strategy	
Product/service positioning	
Pricing	
Distribution	
Promotion and communications	
Action programme, including responsibilities	
People	
Distribution	
Sales outlets	
Direct and indirect communications	

Agents/agencies	
Distance selling	
Discounts	
Commission	
Exports	
Budgets	
Sales	
Margin	
Expenditure	
Cash flow	
Departmental budgets	
Milestones and controls	
Checklist with actions, dates and expected outcomes	
Other considerations	
Professional ethics	
Contractual	
Constraints	
Legal	
International	

There might seem to be a lot of items for consideration in this list. This is because we have tried to give you a thorough checklist and most of them will be relevant to any business.

A brief procedure for marketing planning

Here are some tips for marketing planning:

- Prepare the plan around the same time each year, allowing sufficient time before the major sales and advertising season. The timing could usefully correspond to that of the preparation of the business plan.
- Make sure that the plan has two distinct outlooks: in detail over the next year, and in outline over the next three years.
- Roll the plans into one another, that is update last year's plan to be current (but don't just alter the figures – give it some thought).
- Use a consistent format for the plan so that people get used to reading and using it.
- Invite your colleagues to contribute ideas and suggestions to the plan. This means that people will 'buy into' the ideas and be more likely to use the plan.
- Ensure that you include a set of reporting dates in the plan and issue internal reports that correspond to these dates so that people can see that progress is being made.

CHAPTER 7
Implementing the Marketing Plan

Promotional techniques

Putting the plan into practice means making your marketing ideas work. Once you have put together your plan and set objectives and goals for your company and staff, you must see that the ideas are carried out, that something happens. This is done by telling your customers and potential customers what you have to offer in the way of goods and services – customer communications.

The best method of implementation, in larger organisations, is for the marketing director and manager to direct operations: often this is done through a marketing services unit, who work in collaboration with the sales, manufacturing and other departments. Don't confuse the role of marketing services with that of marketing: the two are very different.

The implementation of the marketing plan is, for many managers, one of the most exciting and interesting phases of marketing. It is also usually the phase that involves the most expenditure, and so can be a nerve-racking time for all concerned. Quite often it is this major expenditure combined with a need to make creative decisions (which by their very nature represent opinions rather than facts) that causes so many rows, resignations and general 'prima donna' behaviour among marketing people.

So,what are the key features of implementation?
They are as follows:

- Communication of the offer
- Managing the relationship with the customer
- Obtaining feedback from the customers as to their views about your firm and your products/services
- Monitoring the implementation to the plan (and taking corrective action if necessary).

Now consider the following case study:

Case study

Stratos Consultants has taken on two new staff recently, both of whom have expertise in environmental management issues. The company sees that there is a lot of consumer concern about the destruction of the tropical rain forests and thinks that it could generate some consultancy business for itself by providing advice to manufacturers in the UK who use tropical hardwoods in their products (an example of such a company is Alto Speakers which uses wooden veneers on its speaker cabinets).

Stratos might take the following steps to generate some business in this area.

Assuming that the facts stated are correct, and that Stratos has analysed the amount of work it wants to obtain, and constructed its target sample accordingly, it might:

- Think of which industries use tropical woods (DIY retailers, lumber merchants, companies making wooden furniture, hi-fi speakers, etc)
- Purchase a list of companies in the target area (for example, by purchasing a mailing list of the relevant standard industrial codes (SIC))
- Put together an outline of the service it plans to offer,

---

and then visit a few companies for the purpose of market research

- Based on the outcome of this, refine its literature to ensure it meets customer needs
- Send out a series of direct mail letters to target clients, phased so that responses can be adequately handled
- When it has carried out its first project, ensure that articles and PR literature are placed in the relevant trade press and journals.

These are all tactical actions, set within an overall strategic framework. If Stratos was to embark on such a course without knowing that there was a demand and interest for the service, it could be a significant waste of time, money and resources.

Communicating with the customer

While the subject of the sales force is not a central topic of this book, and there is much debate whether the sales force is part of the marketing effort or a discipline in its own right, it is certainly a crucial element of the customer communication process.

Customers receive information about products and services in the following manner:

- By contact with representatives of the company
- By seeing advertisements, literature, brochures or mailshots
- By word of mouth from others who use, sell or know of the products and services (third-party information).

The challenge facing those marketing for success is to manage all these communications channels to give the right message, at the right time, but to control them within a budget that is always less than that which might be desired.

Let us look in some detail at each of these channels, some tips and techniques and typical costs and management processes.

Face-to-face contact

For many companies this is generally the easiest area to manage, and perhaps the hardest to do properly. The sales force will usually be 'armed' with a variety of printed literature (brochures, technical manuals, price list, testimonials, etc) and will normally be extensively trained, both in selling techniques and also in the products and services. Actually handling customer communications on a day-to-day basis, however, can be difficult, for the simple reason that sales people have a short-term objective – to get the sale. This can obscure longer-term objectives (for example building market share, or preparing the way for higher value sales), particularly where high levels of commission are involved (as is often the case with life assurance and more recently photocopiers/fax machines and mobile phones).

In smaller firms it is not uncommon for staff to be involved in all aspects of the business, so that the producers or planners are close to the clients or customers. This is not the case, however, as firms grow and staff specialise. It is, therefore, common practice in larger firms for all marketing professionals to spend some time with the sales force out on the road. This can provide benefits over and above the time spent: those brochures that seemed so exciting to you and the design group might seem meaningless or irrelevant to the customer in practice.

Make sure that you spend time with the sales force (where it exists) and listen to what they have to say, and in return try to develop your materials so that the sales people feel comfortable in passing the information on to customers.

Telephone selling

Telephone selling has been used by companies ever since the phone was invented, and is a major part of industrial and consumer sales. You have a responsibility to your customers and to your company to use this powerful method in a responsible, yet effective, way.

For many organisations a good way to manage telephone sales is to set up a central order-processing department and train staff to carry out telesales while orders are being placed ('Thank you for ordering item Y, Senor Garcia, would you like item Z to go with it?').

The telephone section can also be used to canvass for prospects for the sales force and to follow up repeat orders or those that are placed on a regular basis.

While it is true that the sales of high-value products are rarely made solely over the telephone, it is becoming more and more popular to use telecommunications (which includes not only the phone but television, faxes, etc) to manage a large part of the customer interface.

Social conventions determine that for the foreseeable future we will not replace face-to-face contact as the most desirable form of communication, but the spiralling costs of staff and the need for efficiency are forcing many companies to become more inventive about telephone usage. The phenomenal success in the UK of First Direct (a remote banking system launched by Midland Bank) and Direct Line (the remote insurance service of the Royal Bank of Scotland) has forced a competitive response from other banks and insurance companies. Similarly Minitel, in France, which offers a whole range of services through communication channels has also proved very popular.

Many computer systems will now provide details of customers' names, ages, lifestyles and other information, just by entering their phone numbers or postcodes into the telesales operators' PCs. This data revolution has helped to make telemarketing a much more useful tool.

Home shopping via the TV in the USA was one of the big successes in the late 1980s and prompted Sears, Roebuck to stop issuing its (paper) catalogue in 1993.

You may have come across the automatic order taking systems developed by theatres and cinemas where you enter all the details of your order through a telephone keypad. These systems will collect information on what you see and when you buy, and this can be used to develop sales.

As an example, if information was collected on everyone who went to see a Clint Eastwood film, it would enable companies to target potential customers by telephoning to offer videos of his greatest films. Fan clubs, of course, have been doing this in a way for years.

Advertising

This is a complex subject and can only be covered briefly here. The industry is in practice little different from many other service industries, but its exclusive/trendy image is generated by the 'upper' end of the market where the degree of creative input that goes into the work is usually perceived to be higher. This tends to lead to high-profile discussions among clients and agencies (often conducted in public) thus reinforcing the consumer's perception of the industry.

For most people in business, however, advertising means the small ads in papers, *Yellow Pages*, leaflets, local newspapers and local radio stations and cinemas. For some businesses it will also include national press and radio, television and cinema and advertising hoardings.

Going back to first principles, it is worth remembering that the only reason for advertising is to put a message in front of potential (and actual) consumers of your product that gives them the detail they require either to consider or, preferably buy, your product.

This then poses the following questions:

- Which message to put?
- Where to place the advertisement?
- What level of detail should be in it?
- Which consumers should be targeted?

Which message to put

The exact message will depend to an extent on the market research and also the impression that the company feels is best created. You may have noticed that many commercials for beer and lagers are rather light-hearted. Brewers would clearly be foolish to put across a message that 'Our lager gets you very drunk, very quickly', even if this was allowed by the national advertising standards authorities.

This is because, although some people undoubtedly drink for the sole purpose of becoming inebriated, the brewers' research shows that many more do so for the purpose of relaxing in the company of others. Thus the promotion of an image of fun and enjoyment appears to match the aspirations of the target market, which is normally (in the case of lager) younger males.

With smaller businesses ads tend to be simple and direct – 'Use Bloggs dry cleaners, your local friendly service'.

Consider the following: in the UK 'Sonic the Hedgehog 2' by SEGA made more money on the day of its release than the best selling rock CD of 1992 (Simply Red's *Stars*) did in the whole of 1992. Sonic was publicised by a fantastic PR and word-of-mouth campaign.

Where to place the advertisement

The message will also vary considerably according to the medium being used for the campaign. The TV, cinema, press, posters and radio are the main areas that come to mind for advertising, and they all have different characteristics (and costs). A distinction is generally drawn between press and poster adverts and those that can include either sound or moving pictures or both.

As in any area the cost can be prime consideration in the choice of medium, but it would undervalue the sophistication of advertising to suggest that this is the only criteria.

Generally, press advertisements are used for products where the consumer will be interested in substantial amounts of detailed information (for example, lists of products offered by major stores, details of pensions or insurance, job adverts) but can also be used for, say, full page picture adverts.

Press advertisements are generally cheaper to produce than TV adverts and they have shorter deadlines. You can nearly always get an ad in a newspaper, but it is much harder to buy the slot during the main evening news on TV at short notice. A good example of this was when Michael Jackson (then sponsored by Pepsi) was said to be suffering from dehydration, the Coca-Cola company (the major world-wide competitor of Pepsi in soft drinks and cola) ran adverts next day in the press stating that if you were thirsty you should drink Coke – its product.

TV and cinema ads and to a lesser degree radio, have the greatest impact. The use of sound on the radio enables jingles and songs to be joined with words to form a powerful combination message, which is more likely to remain with the listener than just words. Combining sound with vision has created some adverts that must surely rank alongside some works of art. This is all a matter of personal taste, but in the UK the comic adverts for Hamlet cigars in the 1970s and 1980s and the adverts involving Leonard Rossiter and Joan Collins for Cinzano, are widely considered spectacular examples of advertising at its best.

Write down some of the adverts that you both enjoyed and you thought encouraged you to buy the product, and why!

Advertisement	Why it made you consider the product/service

What level of detail
Typically, a 30-second TV or cinema advertisement will have space for only a small amount of information, so the advertiser has to be very clear about the message (called the 'product proposition'). It should be clear, unequivocal and to the point.

Some famous examples where a catch word or phrase has been established include:

Guinness — pure genius

A Mars a day helps you work, rest and play (with a memorable tune)

It's the real thing (Coke) (one of their ad tunes with slightly different words became a number one best-selling single)

Drinka pinta milka day

Beanz meanz Heinz

In the above examples the products are all available through shops, so the advertiser has no need to tell the viewers where to go for the product. However, in the case of more sophisticated products or those only available through specialist outlets, the advertiser will have to include this information as well. For example:

The New Ford Mondeo: at Bloggs Ford of Clapham

McHaggis Marmalade with Whisky: only at Groggles Gourmet Delicatessen

Direct mail and leafleting

Direct mail
Although direct mail generally gets a bad press ('junk mail') it is a very powerful form of customer communication, both in consumer markets and in the business-to-business arena.

Companies planning to use direct mail usually purchase lists of potential consumers (based on, for example, lifestyle or other data) and then use these for mail shots. It is possible to build your own lists (from your own customer data) and then to cross-sell products. Banks particularly do this, for example sending out leaflets from their insurance subsidiary to home owners (from their mortgage records) or car owners (from their loan records). This is a common technique employed by organisations which have a range of products that they feel would interest you.

Lists can be formed by joining your data with purchased data and all lists should be categorised and cross-referenced to ensure that you are only sending mail to people whom you may feel are genuinely interested in what you have to sell – focusing your effort. It would be pointless to offer gardening services to people who live in flats, so it may be appropriate to check if your list can be purged of such data before using it.

There are a number of companies who specialise in offering such list management services, and you can consult them for details.

When the list is ready, a great deal of care and thought must go into a mail shot:

- What you want to say
- How it is presented, and even
- When it is mailed.

Again, this is a specialised subject, but at the very least you should do a small test mailing to see what the reaction is like before you send out 20,000 letters.

And finally, don't forget to contact the Post Office. Not only will they offer you advice on this subject but they have a number of special rates for bulk mailings, plus a number of good ideas on freepost and reply paid envelopes.

Leafleting

Leafleting is really a specialist form of direct mail, except that instead of posting literature (or putting it in magazines/papers as inserts) it is placed directly through the letter box. Many companies offer delivery services and will also advise on targeting mechanisms (for example, based on the post codes of houses, etc).

No doubt you will have been annoyed by people sticking leaflets under your car windscreen wipers, but this can be a very targeted way of offering various services related to car owners (cleaning, valeting, parking, servicing, etc), although it tends not to be so focused most of the time due to insufficient research and planning.

List below some places where you could place leaflets about your products or services (if relevant) so that potential consumers would be likely to see them:

```
_____

_____

_____

_____

_____

_____

_____

_____
```

Public relations (PR)

For many people the image of PR is one of sharp-suited people who accompany pop and film stars around and ensure that anything they say is sanitised, and that only favourable publicity is generated.

In reality, the PR profession is much less glamorous than this and is mainly devoted to ensuring that the press, TV and other media cover stories about clients — favourably.

While newspapers and the TV generally carry news items, there are enormous numbers of trade journals and specialist magazines whose role is to impart specialist information to readers about a topic. To this extent they will often cover stories about new products and contracts and so on for most firms. The key is whether or not the editor thinks the subject will be of general interest to the readers, and the true art of the PR professional is to ensure that stories about the client are prepared and presented in the best possible light and then 'sold' to the media.

There is also a role for PR in managing presentations to the press and or customers and advising generally on media relations.

Some companies choose to handle PR in-house, and some choose external contractors: there are merits to both approaches, but whatever you do ensure that the subject is handled both professionally and responsibly.

Think about the story of the salesman from a double glazing company who is supposed to have upset the editor of a tabloid newspaper, and the editor responded by running a major exposure of the 'Double glazing racket: How So-and-So windows rip you off!' across the centre pages.

Trade shows

Trade shows are, for many companies, an excellent way of showing off their products and services to large groups of customers at once. The largest shows are held in places that have the facilities for this, like the NEC, Olympia and Wembley, in the UK, and the world's most famous book fair held in Frankfurt, Germany, but smaller shows are held every day, all over the country, for example agricultural shows.

The advantages to companies include the fact that nearly all the visitors are potentially interested in your products, and they have come for the purpose of either buying or collecting specific information.

The downside is that all your competitors will be there, probably with stands alongside yours, so people can shop around. In addition it can be quite expensive to hire space and to develop and staff a good stand.

Trade shows are a very popular way to develop into export markets, as the organisers of the show do all the advertising and deal with administration, etc while you concentrate on meeting individual customers.

Think carefully about the potential costs and benefits before you agree to participate.

Directories and other compendiums

The most obvious directory to have your company's name in

is the telephone book, with an advertisement in the *Yellow Pages*.

There are many types of directory (perhaps the most famous being Kompass) which list companies according to the service they provide, their location, etc. Think carefully about the type of advert you want in the directory and what it should say (not too narrow to put people off, not too wide to appear too general). You can certainly do better than the company whose London *Yellow Pages* advert boasts 'We fit most makes of car radio' — hardly the most enticing statement in the world.

There has been considerable growth in recent years of electronic (sometimes called on-line) directories. For a small fee subscribers can use their PCs and a modem (a device that allows you to link into a computer via a phone line) to dial in to the large databases and search for those products and services that are of interest. Some of these cover very large markets (for example Europe or the USA) so they can be a good way to advertise your services to a wider audience.

Resellers

This is a term often used by marketing people to describe those individuals who take products and sell them on without changing or doing anything to them. This group of people encompasses retailers, wholesalers and, of course, any type of trader.

What resellers need is a good understanding of how your product appeals to the target market plus an idea or the contacts to ensure that they can sell more than you can directly (say, for example, by virtue of their own distribution system). They make their money on the (relative) economies of scale from buying and selling in bulk and perhaps providing some additional services (for a price).

The advantage to a business in using them is that it only has to deal with a small number of customers itself and not the mass market. This makes administration simpler and cheaper and does not require campaigns aimed at the general public.

For some companies resellers can make up a substantial

proportion of their turnover, for others it is only a small proportion. Understand your relationship with those customers of yours who resell your products, canvass their needs and help them to satisfy the ultimate consumer, and this will enhance your sales.

Sponsorship and product placement

A rapidly growing area of communications is through sponsorship. (Major golfers or skiers are almost always sponsored by a manufacturer of golf or ski equipment, and use its equipment in tournaments. We have all seen skiing programmes where the skier gets to the bottom of the run and immediately takes off one ski, cleans the snow off, and puts it right in front of the cameras.) For example, in the UK, instead of taking adverts on TV, the brewers of Beamish Stout chose to 'sponsor' the successful 'Inspector Morse' series. They did this because they felt that the values imbued by the show were similar to those of their product – sophistication and intelligence.

List below some TV shows, books or films that you think have commonality with the products listed.

Corn flakes

_____

_____

Vacuum cleaners

_____

_____

Cars

_____

_____

Bars of chocolate

_____

_____

_____

Men's suits

_____

_____

_____

Now do the same for your company's products or services:

_____

_____

_____

Product placement is really a specialist form of PR, whereby manufacturers come to an arrangement with the producers of TV series or films to ensure that the 'stars' are using their products, for example Arnold Schwarzenegger rode a Harley Davidson in _Terminator 2_ as the motorcycle manufacturer liked to link the 'good guy' (a latter day cowboy) with its product.

Managing the relationship with the customer

In the sections above we have discussed ways to communicate your product offer to customers, but once the customer has seen the product and bought it you have to manage the relationship, perhaps by supporting the customer, or at least ensuring that he or she comes back again and again.

The most obvious ways of managing relationships are through areas directly concerned with the product, for example pricing, sales promotion and customer loyalty programmes. The idea behind these techniques is to keep the customer interested and to restrain them from trying out other products.

Of course advertising and PR have a major role to play, but at the point of purchase other techniques are very useful. For example, periodic 'sales' can be good to get customers to purchase items when they might not normally do so. (In the USA sales are virtually a permanent feature of the retail landscape and a similar trend emerged in Europe in the early 1990s as recession bit deep.) Periodic bulk discounts, coupons and free gifts can achieve similar results. Such promotions are not normally announced beforehand to ensure that customers do not take undue advantage of special offers (which after all cost the manufacturer money).

Sales promotion is the term used to describe such activities and they can range in complexity from a free card in a box of tea bags or a model dinosaur in a packet of breakfast cereal (aimed at making children ask their parents to buy the product), through to major exercises like the points given with petrol or Air Miles (one of the largest promotions ever mounted in the UK).

Sales promotions have to be carefully planned as they can go badly wrong. A classic example of this was the 1992 Hoover free flights promotion. The public's interest in purchasing a £100 vacuum cleaner to get air tickets worth several hundred pounds was such that the company was literally overwhelmed with consumers wanting their free gift and it became something of a fiasco. Following a court case, millions of pounds in costs and with many disgruntled customers, the company will certain be more careful about how it constructs promotions in future.

Feedback

In all your communications with customers it is a very good idea to provide a method for them to feedback their ideas and views. This is really an ongoing form of market research.

Techniques can vary from the very simple, like the

questionnaires you find in hotel rooms, and the guarantee forms that you fill in when you buy electrical products (which also ask you a few personal points), to the very complex.

Describe below how you could include something with your product or service to get your customers to give you their views on them:

```
_____

_____

_____

_____
```

More complex plans involve telephoning or calling on customers and questioning them on how they feel about the product or service they have recently bought or used. Sometimes incentives are used to ensure a good response.

People like to be asked their views (for most people their favourite topic of conversation is themselves) but remember that they don't like to be asked and then have their views disregarded. When one of the authors recently bought a new PC, he was telephoned two weeks later to ask how he liked it (very good). He liked it very much and was pleased to be asked for his views, but when he mentioned a small design problem with the disc drive he was told by the researcher 'That's a shame; never mind at least you liked most of it!'

So, make sure that feedback is given the consideration which it deserves and that customers feel that their views have been valued, possibly by replying to specific complaints or by sending news of product updates in response to feedback. As in the following case study:

Case study

When a customer purchases any product at a Cirrus shop, they are given a questionnaire to complete, and a reply paid envelope. If they complete the questionnaire and post it back to Cirrus, Cirrus sends them a voucher worth £2 off their next purchase. This gives the customer a response, something of worth, and encourages him or her to return to Cirrus.

The information from the questionnaires is used by Cirrus to develop its own service and a subsection of it is sold (on computer disks) to a company specialising in selling mailing lists to other companies. The whole process is known in the trade as a self liquidator, as the total cost to Cirrus approaches zero, as the cost of those vouchers redeemed (and not all will be a long way) is balanced against the monies received from the sale of information, and future sales of products.

Monitoring implementation

Virtually every company, large or small, spends a high proportion of its revenues on marketing in its many forms (it could be as high as 5 per cent of all sales, which for large companies could represent millions of dollars, pounds or marks) and so it is mandatory that they follow up how cost effectively this money is being spent. A well-known American, marketing guru, John Wanamaker, once said, 'Of all the money I spend on advertising, I know that half of it is wasted; the trouble is I don't know which half.'

The way to monitor effectiveness and expenditure is by preparing management reports that break down the expenditure against the results – an area of analysis called econometrics – which is not always as straightforward as it sounds.

Below we give examples of some measures of effectiveness

for some types of communications campaign. It is appropriate to consider these in a little detail, if only to give you some ideas about how to prepare your own reports.

Advertising. The normal method is called *reach*: that is to say the advertiser (or its agency) measures how many people in the target market actually saw or read the advert, compared to the plan. The measurement of this differs for each medium used: for advertising on TV the method is known as the television ratings (TVR), which uses market research data and diaries to decide how many people actually saw that advert during 'News at Ten', and how many were in the target market. For newspapers and magazines, you can look at the number of sales of the publication, and then look at how many people read it (surprisingly these numbers can be very different – for example for every copy of the *Reader's Digest* sold it is estimated, or claimed by the publishers, that the numbers of those reading it are actually getting on for double figures).

Where adverts have a direct response mechanism (for example, 'Phone this number now') then the response can be directly measured.

A further method of analysis is to look at the sales of your product in the last comparable period and decide how much the advertising has increased them, although this is only really relevant in consumer markets.

Direct mail. The normal way of measuring this is to look at the response rate: how many letters were sent out, how many replies were received, and thence, how many sales.

Public relations (PR). In PR, a common method is to work out how many column inches of coverage have been generated by a press release or promotion and then compare this to the cost if you had actually bought the space. Again, the number of contacts generated can be a good measure.

Salesforce visits. It is appropriate to keep a record of salesforce visits and the outcome of these in terms of orders, order size, etc. Many companies operate very sophisticated systems of salesforce monitoring and control.

Some techniques are quite specialised, can be complex in execution, and the results frequently capable of interpretation in a variety of manners, so it is a good idea to get some expert advice.

CHAPTER 8
Looking Ahead

It is often said that the difference between marketing and sales is simply one of time-scale: selling is about getting an order today, marketing about securing orders for next year.

This has to be borne in mind when you have completed the marketing planning task for the year, the document is sitting on the desk, and the staff are raring to go.

Just like preparations for Christmas or painting the Forth Bridge, as soon as the plan is written and the actions started, it is time to start the process over again. Most companies use what is known as a rolling plan to control their business. The marketing plan has two distinct timescales:

- A one-year, detailed plan
- A three-to five-year sketched-out plan.

Every year, the new plan should take the three-to five-year plan and, after working out how well things have gone, 'roll' parts of this into the next year's detailed plan (not forgetting to add to the long-term parts of the plan).

This process is extremely important as marketing is about setting strategic goals for yourself and your company, and although you cannot be anything like as detailed as you might want to be about the distant future (unless your company sells crystal balls that is) you must still consider it.

The diagram 'Company strategy' on page 105, shows a typical strategy chart for a company. The size of the circles represents the company's turnover in absolute terms, and the diagram shows that the company wants to get much larger in 1995 (principally by adding to its product range and thus sales, even at the expense of profits). However, by 1996 this strategy has led to the company splitting into two divisions, both with even larger product ranges, but much smaller turnover, although at high levels of profit.

You should try to plot this kind of strategy diagram for your business, it is not hard especially as it is only indicative, and it can help you to appraise the future progress of your business. Plot where you are now, compared with where you want to be. When you have done this, list the marketing actions that will take you there.

Long-term customers

It is also worth mentioning that longer-term marketing ultimately pays bigger dividends than short term, as existing customers are generally easier to sell to. This is because they have tried your products or services and (assuming that they were favourably impressed) know the standard of quality, price, etc. They also require less marketing effort as you do not have to prove who you are, nor tell them where you are but only that you have another product or service that you think they might be interested in. Think of all the direct mail that you get from all the bodies to which you subscribe, and the companies from which you have bought or use in some form or another.

Banks worldwide are currently falling over themselves to acquire or build in-house insurance expertise so that they can sell those products and services to their existing banking customers, using their existing distribution networks. (This was also, however, the strategy underlying the scramble for brokers and estate agencies which ended in disaster for most.)

People tend to be quite loyal in where they go for products and services, and maintaining the client contact and therefore

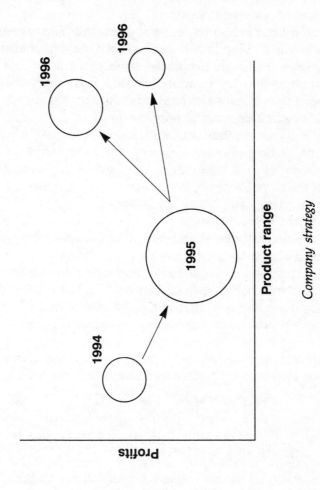

Company strategy

their 'goodwill' is a very important part of marketing. Winning market share (which is in nearly all plans) is achieved only by persuading people to change their choice from your rivals or by convincing them to buy a new product or service (yours). If you get them interested enough to change they usually remain loyal to their new suppliers.

For example people rarely change their bank, mainly because it is difficult, but if they do they almost never change again, and almost never back to a previous bank. That is why banks try to woo potential new clients at the earliest ages, that is school leavers and university students, banking on this (often life-long) loyalty.

Another method of building up consumer loyalty is via store cards. These are very effective ways of ensuring customers visit your store. The card is only available for use in the store (or chain) and enables many purchases to be made with great ease. Many cards also offer credit with the cards and the interest charged brings in extra income. The cards also provide very useful information about spending patterns and can be used to target customers for special promotions, etc.

The graph on page 107 shows why longer-term customers are more profitable over time as you can capitalise on your initial investment in gaining the customer by selling them more products, replacements, referrals and so on.

On a final note, let us leave you with a quote from Michael Porter, famous strategist and author of *Competitive Strategy*

'...if you misdefine the market, you probably miss opportunities and underestimate the competition, which means that the strategic decisions at the level of the business may also be wrong...'

What Porter means is that the foundation of all marketing lies in understanding your customers and the competition (market research) and if you get this wrong all your marketing will be to no avail. Any decision made on the basis of inadequate or poor information will be totally flawed and could lead to disaster. Therefore, carry out your market research, formulate a

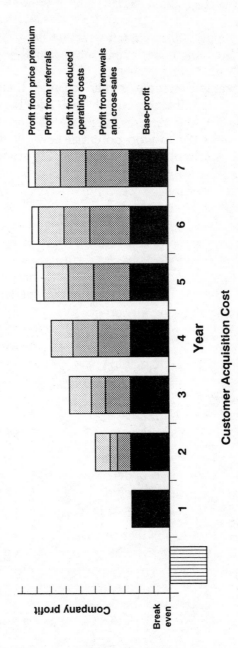

Customer retention: why customers are more profitable over time

strategy and plan, communicate to the customers, and then go back to the beginning again and review your marketing constantly.

Apply the principles we have set out here, get some expert advice where you need it and success in the market will be yours.

Useful Addresses

Advertising Association
Abford House
15 Wilton Road
London SW1V 1NJ
Tel 071-828 2771

Chartered Institute of Marketing
Moor Hall
Cookham
Maidenhead
Berkshire SL6 9QH
Tel: 0628 524922
Fax: 0628 819195

Direct Marketing Association UK
Haymarket House
1 Oxendon Street
London SW1Y 4EE
Tel 071-321 2525

Institute of Practitioners in Advertising
44 Belgrave Square
London SW1X 8QS
Tel 071-235 7020

Market Research Society
15 Northburgh Street
London EC1V 0AH
Tel 071-490 4911

Further Reading from Kogan Page

Marketing

Everything You Need to Know About Marketing, P Forsyth
How to Get on in Marketing, N Hart, N Waite
How to Market Books, A Baverstock
How to do Marketing Research, P Hague and P Jackson
How to Improve Your Marketing Copy, I Linton
Know Your Customers, J Curry
Marketing Communications, P Smith
Practical Marketing, D Bangs
Sales Promotion, J Cummins

Advertising

Great Advertising Campaigns, N Ind
The New How to Advertise, K Roman and J Maas

Public Relations

Effective PR Management, P Winner
Public Relations Case Studies, S Black
Targeting Media Relations, D Wragg
The Essentials of Public Relations, S Black
The PR Business, Q Bell